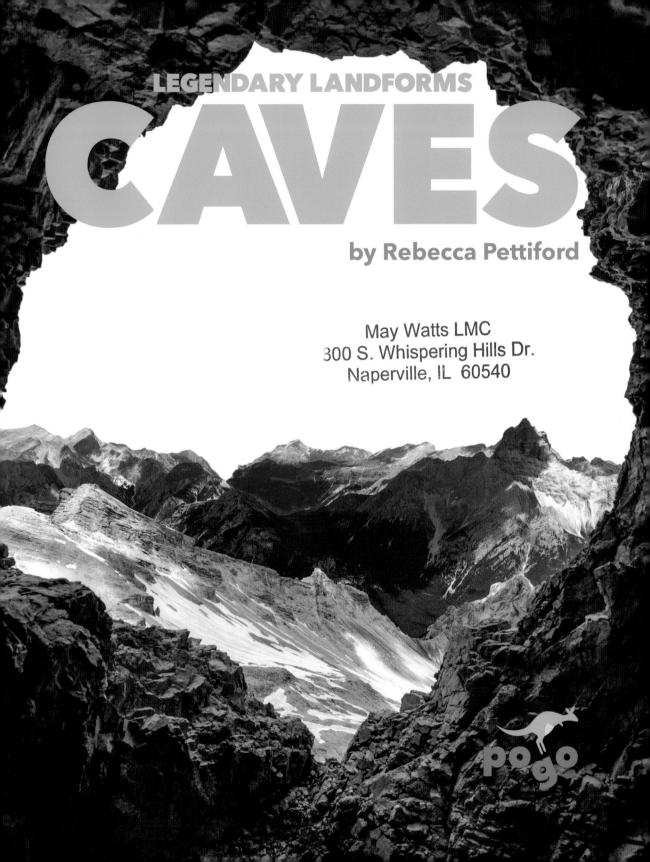

LEGENDARY LANDFORMS
CAVES

by Rebecca Pettiford

pogo

Ideas for Parents and Teachers

Pogo Books let children practice reading informational text while introducing them to nonfiction features such as headings, labels, sidebars, maps, and diagrams, as well as a table of contents, glossary, and index.

Carefully leveled text with a strong photo match offers early fluent readers the support they need to succeed.

Before Reading

- "Walk" through the book and point out the various nonfiction features. Ask the student what purpose each feature serves.
- Look at the glossary together. Read and discuss the words.

Read the Book

- Have the child read the book independently.
- Invite him or her to list questions that arise from reading.

After Reading

- Discuss the child's questions. Talk about how he or she might find answers to those questions.
- Prompt the child to think more. Ask: Have you ever been to a cave? Where was it? What kinds of things did you see there?

Pogo Books are published by Jump!
5357 Penn Avenue South
Minneapolis, MN 55419
www.jumplibrary.com

Library of Congress Cataloging-in-Publication Data

Names: Pettiford, Rebecca, author.
Title: Caves / by Rebecca Pettiford.
Description: Minneapolis, MN: Jump!, Inc., [2017]
Series: Legendary landforms | "Pogo Books are published by Jump!." | Audience: Ages 7-10.
Includes bibliographical references and index.
Identifiers: LCCN 2016046946 (print)
LCCN 2016047841 (ebook) | ISBN 9781620317075 (hardcover: alk. paper) | ISBN 9781620317457 (pbk.)
ISBN 9781624965845 (ebook)
Subjects: LCSH: Caves–Juvenile literature.
Landforms–Juvenile literature.
Classification: LCC GB601.2 .P48 2017 (print)
LCC GB601.2 (ebook) | DDC 551.44/7–dc23
LC record available at https://lccn.loc.gov/2016046946

Editor: Kirsten Chang
Book Designer: Leah Sanders
Photo Researcher: Leah Sanders

Photo Credits: NNehring/Getty, cover; DreamPictures/ Jensen Walker/Getty, 1; Robert_Ford/iStock, 3; Tatiana Kolesnikova/Getty, 4; Marisa Estivill/Shutterstock, 5; DESIGN PICS INC/National Geographic Creative, 6-7; kotangens/Thinkstock, 8-9; SV Production/ Shutterstock, 10; Tristan Savatier/Getty, 11; Frontpage/ Shutterstock, 12-13; Santi Rodriguez/Shutterstock, 14-15; Doug Meek/Getty, 16-17; Zack Frank/ Shutterstock, 18; David S. Boyer and Arlan R. Wiker/ National Geographic Creative, 19; Dante Fenolio/Getty, 20-21; Imgorthand/iStock, 23.

Printed in the United States of America at Corporate Graphics in North Mankato, Minnesota.

TABLE OF CONTENTS

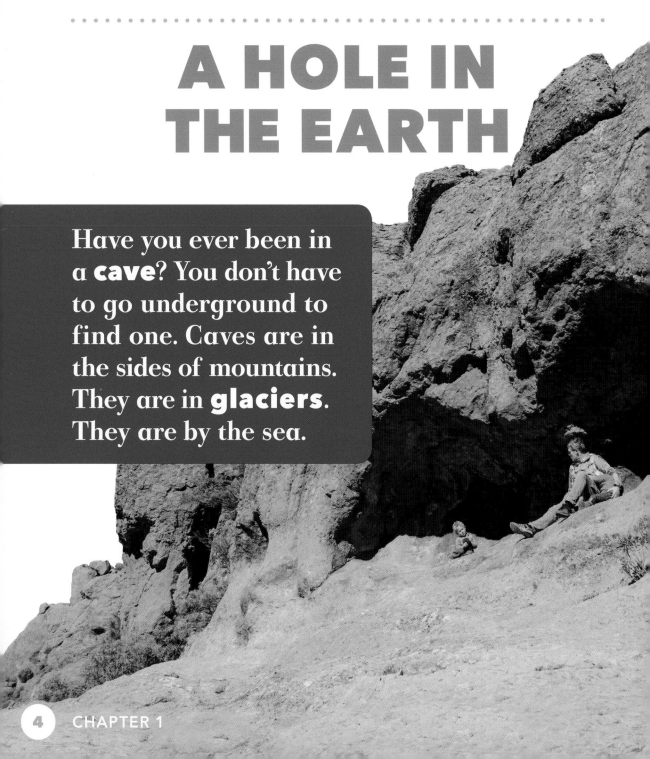

CHAPTER 1

A HOLE IN THE EARTH

Have you ever been in a **cave**? You don't have to go underground to find one. Caves are in the sides of mountains. They are in **glaciers**. They are by the sea.

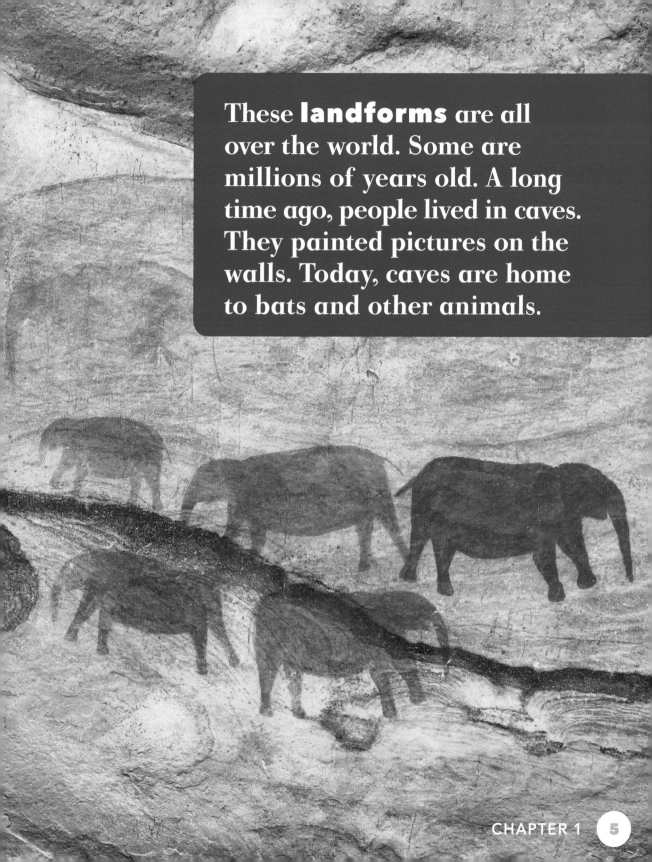

These **landforms** are all over the world. Some are millions of years old. A long time ago, people lived in caves. They painted pictures on the walls. Today, caves are home to bats and other animals.

There are several types of caves. Sea caves form when ocean waves pound against rock.

Ice caves are formed by melted streams. They cut tunnels under glaciers.

Another kind of cave is formed by **lava**. After hot lava flows from **volcanoes**, it cools. It hardens on the surface. Under the surface, lava still flows. When it flows away, a lava cave remains.

DID YOU KNOW?

Glow worms live in some New Zealand caves. Their sticky webs hang from the ceiling. They trap insects to eat.

CHAPTER 2

INSIDE A CAVE

The most common type of cave is a **limestone** cave.

How do these caves form? Rain absorbs **carbon dioxide** from the air. It drips through the soil. It picks up more carbon dioxide.

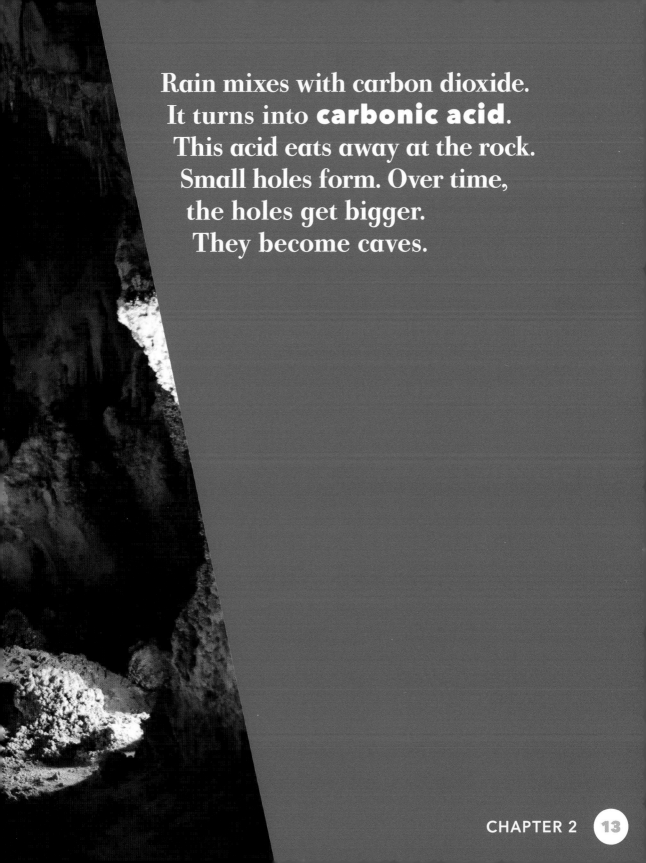

Rain mixes with carbon dioxide.
It turns into **carbonic acid**.
This acid eats away at the rock.
Small holes form. Over time,
the holes get bigger.
They become caves.

The **solution** drips. It creates cave formations. When a drop dries on the ceiling, it leaves a bit of **calcite crystal**. These crystals build up. They hang from the ceiling. These are called **stalactites**.

Drops also fall to the cave floor. They dry. **Stalagmites** form.

stalactite

stalagmite

When a stalactite meets a stalagmite, it forms a column. These formations can be very tall. How tall? Some can reach 200 feet (62 meters). That is the height of five giraffes!

How is a column made?
1 Carbonic acid drips through a limestone ceiling.
2 Calcite crystals build up. A stalactite forms.
3 Drops fall to the floor. A stalagmite forms.
4 The stalactite and stalagmite meet. A column forms.

1   2   3   4

☐ = limestone
■ = calcite crystals

CHAPTER 3

MAMMOTH CAVE

Today people tour caves and **caverns** all over the world.

MAMMOTH CAVE NATIONAL PARK

A World Heritage Site and International Biosphere Reserve

Mammoth Cave is the longest system of caves in the world. It is in Kentucky. It has more than 400 miles (643 kilometers) of passages.

Mammoth Cave is home to strange animals such as albino shrimp and Southern cavefish. These animals evolved to live in the dark. They don't have eyes. Their skin is colorless.

Would you like to see columns and cavefish? You can visit this legendary landform. Plan a trip to Mammoth Cave!

DID YOU KNOW?

People who explore caves are called spelunkers. Exploring a cave can be unsafe. You should go with an experienced guide.

Southern cavefish

TRY THIS!

MAKE A STALACTITE

You can make a cave stalactite at home!

What You Need:

- two glass jars that are the same size
- hot water
- 1 cup baking soda
- washcloth
- scissors
- string
- plate

1. Fill two glass jars with hot water. Leave about an inch (2.5 centimeters) of space at the top of each jar.

2. Add ½ cup baking soda to each jar. Stir until dissolved.

3. Fold the washcloth into a triangle. Roll it tightly.

4. Cut three lengths of string. Tie the cloth on both ends and in the middle. Snip the extra string off the knots.

5. Put each end of the cloth into a jar. The ends of the cloth must touch the bottoms of the jars. Pull the center of the cloth down. It should dip towards the table. Put a plate under it.

6. Let it sit for three to five days. Check on it every day. Soon, you will see a stalactite form. After five days, you should see a pillar that goes from the cloth to the plate!

GLOSSARY

calcite crystal: A hard mineral that is either white or colorless.

carbon dioxide: A colorless and odorless gas present in the air that dissolves in water to form carbonic acid.

carbonic acid: A weak acid that eats away rock.

cave: A large, natural hole underground or in the side of a hill or cliff.

caverns: Caves that have most of their open spaces underground.

glaciers: Large, slow-moving bodies of ice.

landforms: Natural features of Earth's surface.

lava: Melted rock from a volcano.

limestone: Rock made from the remains of ancient shells and marine animals.

solution: A liquid in which something has been dissolved.

stalactites: A pillar that hangs from a cave's ceiling.

stalagmites: A pillar that rises from the ground of a cave.

volcanoes: Mountains with a hole in their tops or sides that force out rocks, ash, and lava.

INDEX

TO LEARN MORE

Learning more is as easy as 1, 2, 3.

1) Go to www.factsurfer.com

2) Enter "legendarycaves" into the search box.

3) Click the "Surf" button to see a list of websites.

With factsurfer, finding more information is just a click away.